Voyages

Ross W Smith

**PAPERBACK
EXCHANGE
131 Vesta
Reno, Nevada 89502
WE SELL - WE TRADE**

Copyright © 2006 Ross Smith
All rights reserved.
ISBN: 1-4196-3222-1
Library of Congress Control Number : 2006902262

To order additional copies, please contact us.
BookSurge, LLC
www.booksurge.com
1-866-308-6235
orders@booksurge.com

Voyages
Poems

Ross Smith

2006

Voyages

TABLE OF CONTENTS PAGE

Nature and Environment	1
Seven Poems on Love	39
Voyages	49
Twenty Five Ramblings	67
Cities	77
Politics, War, Revolution and Horror	95
Religion, Politics and Hate	121
Living and Thinking	133
End Notes	171

Dedicated To My Wife
Vicki Toy-Smith

NATURE AND ENVIRONMENT

THE MOUNTAIN TRAIL

The mountain trail into the distance,
A winding snake into the sun,
Never straight but always turning,
Always filled with some strange substance,
Where, oh where, does this trail lead?
Why does it always give a yearning?

A burning thought of mystery,
Of brightest shining armor,
Always some great history,
To see inside the further moor,
Along a path that's never true.

Mystic shrines of endless dreaming,
Of a trail as yet obscure,
Gives us life and gives us death,
As a nightingale that's singing,
And with steps that are unsure,
We seek the end,
But, is it only death?

THE DUST DEVIL AND THE EAGLE

The dust devil spun across the desert valley,
Sending dust and pebbles into the air,
And sending small creatures
Scurrying from their perches,

Overhead an eagle circled
In motion counter to the devil's spin,
Looking for prey.
Spotting a rodent seeking cover,
It dove triumphantly.

What is this coupling of a living being
With a non-living devil?

LIFTING CLOUDS

See now the clouds,
Luminous in sunlight,
Ominous before a storm,
Erupt with rain
Walk wet and watch the clouds rupture,
On a path so sure,
That deviation is impractical,
Rush forward, to the stone cabin,
And hide,
Wait until the clouds shine again,
And you will experience rapture,
Seek then riches,
Made of tin on a far off peak,
See the shine of sunlight,
Among the lifting clouds,
All not to be sought without feeling,
Never to be possessed, except by seeing.

THE DESERT

Desert nights, always flights,
Sagebrush blooms come the doom,
Rocky sights sometimes fright,
Ghosts seem to be a tomb.

Misty sights of dust at night,
Run around with all their might,
Coyotes howl, always warring,
As if to say "this is a warning".

The cholla pricks and bites,
And makes shapes unreal,
What terror is this light so bright,
This fear you can feel.

Death is here and is there,
Why come to a place as here?
For fear is life,
And here is life.

THE HILLS AND FORESTS

One morning the sun was so bright,
The sky so blue we read to one another,
The pages burned our minds,
And we saw red surrounded by blue,
So we looked into the sun,
And returned to our book.

The day grew cold and still we read on,
A leaf blew off the nearest tree,
We should have gone inside,
But though the land was cold,
It was clean and serene,
The leaves always that which clings,
And that which feeds.

Come, and walk with me along the forest path,
Read to me some more,
Smell the pines,
Let me lead you or I will follow.
And when it is dark you will see the sun.

But the wind was very great.
Where are the leaves going?

TRANQUILITY

When shadows fall upon the mountain lake
And day is spent and alpenglow on nearby
Peaks and domes turns bright,
Then darkens to a deep red and finally dissipates,
A hush is cast upon the land.

I, sampling brandy, am at peace with the world.
Everyday turmoil is thrust from my mind
And I feel tranquility in this sensual moment.

BACKPACKING

We walked along a mountain path,
Heavy burden and all.
We climbed endless stairs of stone
Past granite ramparts,
And past churning water.

Mists from the waterfalls,
Cooled us occasionally,
Although the sun bore down on us relentlessly,
Resulting in beads of perspiration.

Our packs grew seemingly heavier.
Where is the end of the trail?
Where are we to spend the night?

The shining peaks grow closer,
Radiating warmth although the air grows colder.

What is it that so beckons us
To the highest ramparts of such rough mountains?
Do we seek the mountains for themselves?
Or do we seek ourselves?
Does the hard challenge free us?

DESPOILED BY GREED AND NEGLECT

Riding high above the clouds,
We see not the city below,
And are free of its proud contamination.
We see not the ruin of the forest.

Descending, we walk through a land despoiled,
And think of past forests preserved by natural events.
What is it that drives man to despoil his nest?
Is it greed for riches?
Is it simple neglect?

NATURE AND MAN

Don't all depend on
And are coupled with physical forces of nature?
Lava flows as a destructive force,
But it replenishes land and nourishes man.

Rivers destroy landscapes,
But deposit silt turning to soil,
And on and on goes the intimate relations,
Between creatures and physical acts of nature.

THE FOOTHILL CANYON

On a hot sunny day
Manzanita clings to rocky slopes
Above the tumbling river
Rushing downward over jagged rocks,
Interrupted by occasional pools,
Where trout dart from sunny runs to dark recesses.

Vultures circle overhead in lazy spirals,
Looking for carrion.
A deer sleeps within a cool clump of trees,
Higher up a mountain lion also sleeps,
Stretched out in limp position,
Waiting for the night's hunt.

A man clambers down the rocky slopes.
While all creatures ignore him.
Is he seeking the fish?
Or is he out for adventure?
Or merely for solitude and contemplation?
He sits on a large rock just above the churning water,
And watches trout and vultures dart and circle.
Then, he, too, stretches out and naps.

THE DEVIL'S THROAT

The Devils Throat is but a name though grand
Of a waterfall, part of *Cataratas do Iguaçu*
Beautiful beyond comprehension in a land
Of subtropical forest by the Iguaçu
Between Brazil and Argentina and of mists
That form rainbows above the roaring water

A place of romance and an inspiration
Of the beauty nature does provide
For all who can believe in inspiration
Derived from what the physical must provide

What is to be learned from such exotic places?
Can it be the simple knowledge of their existence?
That the world is multifaceted and glorious
And beauty exists in bountiful amounts
Throughout the world if we simply seek it.

BEAUTIFUL VISTAS-PAST AND PRESENT

I remember the long walk to Crescent Lake
And Buena Vista Crest
As if it was yesterday, not sixty years ago.
I remember other trips of equal beauty,
Some last month, some decades ago.
They run into each other,
I can not tell which preceded which,
For all are filled with timeless enchantment,
And with memories of magic and rapture.

What is it about wilderness that so enraptures?
With the feeling of being one with nature,
And all the creatures, plants, rocks and water.

I always feel so alive and at home in such places,
In the mountains, in the desert, near the sea,
Everywhere where wildness dominates,
And man is present as one with all the land.

SIERRA NEVADA FRONT

The branches in the pine wave
In a frantic manner-a precursor of the Zepher
Lenticular clouds overhead dramatically sculptured

At first warm, the compression before the storm
Over the mountain front
The lower clouds gathering covering peaks

Rain showering the countryside followed by snow
A quick return to sunshine, the peaks covered with white
The valley pines green and fresh

On the passes the pines and firs covered with snow
Sparkling in the sunlight.

TWO POEMS, ONE A SENRYU[1]

In a recess in the Flathead Alps
Prisoner Lake stands dark
Forever a prisoner of the mountains

Among Flathead Alps
Prisoner Lake appears dark
Mountain prisoner

BIG SUR

Looking down from the small meadow hanging
In cliffs above the breakers on rocks pounding
The crashing of ocean onto land
Is nowhere more powerful than the pounding
Of Pacific Ocean onto the Big Sur Coast
Mountains with immense boldness rising
To jagged peaks with redwood canyons cutting
Into cliffs with chaparral covering

Trails steeply rising in a manner curving
Up into the rugged mountains containing
Deer, turkeys, mountain lions, wild boars
All in harmony living and co-existing
With one another and among
The redwoods and live oaks
With poison oak and pines protruding
From everywhere producing food for the living
Creatures of the coast and on the crags clinging
To life in great splendor the earth singing

Small rivers and creeks tumbling and sparkling
In sunlight and in rainy mists hanging
Over the mountains and the surf dancing
To tunes of the grey whales singing
Their praises of the enchanted coast
And mountain kingdom,
A climax of mountains and ocean thundering
Beauty everywhere
Sparkling in the sunlight and mists
As nowhere else.

A DAY IN THE DRAKENSBERG[2]

Dawn cloudless sun brilliantly shining
Walking along the contour path
The day reddening
And hazy with the nearby
Cathedral Range disappearing
Mysteriously as I left the path heading
Toward a Bushman Cave with paintings
Of a thousand animals and men running

I stopped in the cave and with awe was gazing
At the three tone Bushman paintings
Long abandoned by the Bushmen running
From invaders from above and below seeking
Their expulsion, then I felt the
Bushman presence continuing
In some mysterious manner
And I left almost running

Back toward the contour path
With the sky ever reddening
As I reached the path the color of the reddening
Atmosphere ominous and I ran faster starting
To feel evermore the strange
Presence overpowering
Redness was everywhere and as I approaching

My camp the sky now suddenly blackening
With a darkness blacker than night

And I almost screaming
As I fumbled toward camp not seeing
When the rain started black sending
A rain of mud onto all plants
And myself splattering
Myself and my tent with a mud covering.

I crawled into the tent muddy and shaking
With something unknown and fearing
What might happen next and seeking?
Was I the Bushmen spirits seeking?
Yet in less than an hour the clouds dissipating
And the sun again brilliantly shining.

GHOST FORESTS

Where has the great *Parana Pine* forest
Of Southern Brazil gone?
Where have the great White Pine Forests
Of Michigan and Wisconsin gone?
Is there anything left of them
In houses as beams or elsewhere?
Are even stumps left in Southern Brazil
Or the Upper Midwest?

Traveling across the *Serra Gaucho*
One sees grassy lands with cattle
And occasional small clumps
Of the remaining *Araucaria* forest
Nearing Itaimbizinho one has no notion
Of what is to be seen.
Suddenly the rolling high plain of the Serra
Ends in the great *Aparado da Serra*
Narrow, thousands of feet deep
With vertical sides and waterfalls falling into it.
And remnant *Parana pines*
As parasols lining the rim
The rolling plains are still exciting today

Yet what was the seemingly endless expanse
Of the great *Araucaria* forest like?
But now only the few remnants
Of the ghost forest
Remind us of that magnificence

In Michigan or Wisconsin one now travels
Miles through pleasant farmland
Where only remnants of the great
White Pine Forests remain
And sometimes second growth
Forests of pine and birch trees

Crossing various streams
Such as the Au Sable one is reminded
Of the plentiful grayling
That once graced these streams
Now gone from silt
From the rape of the forest
Now the great forest of *Pinus stroubus*
Can only be imagined
Now but a ghost forest
Clear-cut to remnants

Yet many other ghost forests
Exist throughout the world
Why has man been so determined?
To completely destroy such forests?
Could not some sizable tracts of forests
Be left uncut?
Why leave only ghosts?

Has man in any way learned lessons?
From this past destruction
Today the great tropical forests
Of the world are cut
At an ever increasing rate,

The Amazon rain forest,
The forests of Borneo
And many other forests.
How can this be slowed if not stopped?

ODE TO PINES

Cone bearing they are and often symmetrical.
Green always and above other trees of the forest.
They live in wet swamps
And on dry barren mountain slopes,
In cold tree line landscapes and hot desert hills.

Their pungent odor permeates the
Forest and the back yard.
Their litter covers the forest floor
And softens footfalls.
Walking beneath them is as in a cathedral,
With sounds muted
Unless a squirrel or jay complains of visitors.

We are in awe of the largest of them,
And thrilled by the ageless presence
Of the most twisted of them
And enthralled by their green
And sometimes grey-green presence.

As we walk silently among their presence,
We may be surprised by the lovely pine grosbeak,
Or by a pine marten seeking prey
All in harmony with the pines and meadow glens.
If wind appears the pines bend and shake,
And sound like running water

In the back yard the pines bend with the wind
And are precursors of shaking rafters inside.

With the wind, the rain may start, freshening the trees,
And increasing the pine scent of the air.

Will the pines be forever,
And will they ever not be with us?
What awful event could take them
And the rest of nature from us?

Yet population pressure
Could accelerate the loss of forests
And pines would not be spared.
But the world without pines
 Is unimaginable.

FROZEN LAKES

Finland is a land of lakes, frozen
In late fall and winter with sun low on the horizon.
Birch trees without leaves, evergreen pines
Stately in the frozen light and dark
At night with the moon casting shadows

The towns bustle with shoppers pushing
Hand sleds or walking with caution
The lighted outdoor park looking sparkling
Amid the relics of past mining works
And a pick up hockey game progressing.

LITTLE LAKES VALLEY

The trail, once a mine road
To the pine creek mine
Starts up a moderate slope
Then opens to views of the great peaks
At the head of Little Lakes Valley
Bear Creek Spire, Mount Dade,
Mount Abbot and Mount Mills
With Mount Morgan to the side
Small glaciers look down on the narrow valley
And shine in sunlight

Lakes and meadows in great profusion
Box, Mack, Grass, Long, Chicken Foot
As the easy Trail wanders to Morgan Pass
Accompanied by branches of Rock Creek
And Gem Lakes at the base of the great peaks
Flowers grace rocky places
The very essence of the High Sierra
Is Little Lakes Valley

GIBB RIVER ROAD

Starting at Kununurra where pink diamonds
From the Argyle mine nearby are displayed.
A gravel road into the Kimberley going westward
Crossing streams impassible during the wet
But low with billabongs during the dry
Alternate areas of flat covered by light forests
Of small eucalyptus and acacias
And low hills to cross

A side road leads to the burning
Red Bungle Bungles
And their beehive shapes with palm canyons
Dry streams with deep pools below waterfalls
Aboriginal paintings, sun and bush flies
Monitor lizards and birds galore

Another side road leads to El Questro Station
With cabbage leaf eucalyptus trees
With a gorge filled with water
And multitudes of fish
With fresh water crocodiles aplenty
On the gorge walls, rock wallabies abound
And aboriginal paintings of crocodiles
Elsewhere barramundi fishing excels
Nearby are gorges with hot springs

Further along a side road
Leads to Mount Elizabeth Station
With beautiful aboriginal paintings

And the southernmost of the Bradshaw paintings
With human figures with sashes often dancing
With an age of 40,000 years
Who were the painters of such beauty?

Yet further along is another road
Leading to Mountain Station
And then into a remote countryside
With a stream with a large billabong
And more fish and freshies
Exotic plants line the shore
And are home to Parrots,
Galahs, Kookaburras and King Cockatoos

Then the King Leopold Ranges are crossed
Windjana Gorge beckons with its limestone cliffs
Turning brilliantly red in the sunset.
Nearby Tunnel Creek flows a mile
Through the limestone range
With a spring within the mountain
From the darkness the stream
Glows when the end is reached
At the tunnel's end and a pool
Surrounded by Eucalyptus

As the road's end nears there is a
Hollow baobab tree
That was once used as a jail.
And the great Fitzroy is crossed
In the dry a small stream with giant billabongs
In the wet carrying more water that the Nile

Finally the road's end is reached
At Broome where pearl fishers ply their trade.

Can it be that there are
Two types of people in the world
Those who have traveled the Gibbs River Road
And those who have not.

DOWN INTO THE CANYON

Down into the canyon
The start cold among the pines and firs
Steep, rocky and filled with broken branches,
Forest littler and fallen rocks
The temperature rising with descent
Various shrubs increasing
Deciduous oaks, western dog wood
Then evergreen oaks and poison oak

Mosquitoes, small flies increasing
Temperature soaring
As the river is reached
Small waterfalls heard
Bear spore along the trail
The tumbling river is seen
With large pools and trout
Evidence of earlier high water

A journey into different life zones
Displaying the wonders of the canyon
And its challenge is as a journey of one's life

LACK OF CARE

The crimson sunset turned the creek red
As if the mountain was bleeding
And should not the mountain bleed?
From what has been done to her forests
By clearcutting
And to her slopes by rupture through
Uncontrolled mining followed by neglect

The suburbs grow uncontrollably
At the expense of forest and cropland
Asphalt consumes meadows and wetlands
Toxic discharges foul the rivers
Auto exhausts foul the atmosphere
Uncontrolled vehicles befoul the land

What is it about us that cares so little?
About where we live
And so little about what we leave
To our progeny

CLARITY OF MOUNTAIN AND MIND

Looking across the High Sierra Peaks
A glacier shining in the clear air
Appeared something one could touch
Although thirty miles away

Such clarity is rare in our minds
As minds are often confused
By the awful falseness
That is continuously fed us
By our leaders-be they our Supervisors
Or our National Leaders
All for their greater glory
Be it nothing but arrogant selfness

How then can we achieve the clarity?
Such as one sees among the high peaks
When cluttered by the vain and ambitious

ACROSS THE VALLEYS AND THE MOUNTAINS

Driving eastward across desert valleys
And pine covered mountains,
Each vista is a revelation of infinite
Distance and infinite longing.
Distant clouds above distant mountains
Appear as angels and the dark mountains
Seem ominous although inviting.

What wonders do these mountains hold?
Are they waterless or do small streams
Sparkle downward through aspen and pine?
In the higher crags do small lakes
Shimmer in the sun and brood under clouds?
Are there patches of snow
Remaining from last winter's storms?

Are there bold limestone outcrops?
And does the limestone soak up
Water from the winter snows?
Will the distant clouds bring soaking
Showers amidst bold lightning strikes?
Or will the clouds dissipate and bring nothing.

Have the winter storms
Rejuvenated grassy meadows,
Where springs give rise to trickling streams?
Are birds now building nests

Among the leafing aspens?
Have the squirrels started nests
And look to finding stored pine nuts?

SUNSET TO SUNSET

As we drive across the mountains on a late fall day,
We drive directly into the setting sun.
And as it sinks into the horizon
It becomes ever redder.

As it sinks below the horizon it becomes diffuse
Leaving a redness in the sky,
And if we a can look back at the mountains
We see then bathed in alpenglow.

As the light dwindles and becomes a mere ghost,
Night ascends and blankets foothills and the valley.
Stars appear giving sparkle to the scene
Moonrise casts faint shadows onto the land.
And night time creatures dessert their sanctuaries,
To forage and hunt for their survival.
Only sunrise ends their night time wanderings.

Daybreak brings to life the awakening creatures
Who have been dormant through the night
And they start their daytime tasks.
As the sun rises they start their day time bustle.
The City in the Valley awakes
And hides them in her bosom.
Men and women toil in nameless offices
And in the many streets, hurrying to complete
Their given tasks among the concrete structures
Past lunch they nod their heads,
But carry on their appointed burdens,

Until the day begins to wane
Bringing forth another sunset.
We then start back across the mountains,
To complete the cycle of life,
And looking toward more days and nights.

.

WILL YOU WALK WITH ME?

Will you walk with me to magical places
In the mountains and in my mind?
Let us think of deep blue lakes,
Shining in the bright sunlight,
Or ominous under clouds.

Do you think as I do about the
Magic of each moment when the clouds
Pass in front of the sun and change light into dark,
Or as sun sets the calmness of the lake,
And reflections of the mountain spires
Mirrored in the lake.

Does your spirit soar into those spires,
Although rooted to the ground?
While in the spires my mind explores new ideas,
Which I take to bed with me and whenever I wake,
Adds puzzles to my life and a thirst for knowledge.

Then, in the morning as the sun
Bursts over the high ridge,
And a new day dawns and offers new adventures.
We walk along a rocky path toward those spires.
We see as we approach them that
They are not magical, but simply rock outcrops.

Yet they are magical for they
Have brought us to this spot,
And we can look back down to the lake

Which now appears as even more enchanted
And magical in its deep recess.
And the surrounding forest is dark and black.
We also see further peaks
Off into the purple distance.
These peaks now in turn beckon us.

They shimmer in the early morning light
All decked out in snow patches and barren rock.
Forests lower on their slopes appear as a distant land,
With unknown creatures and little trodden tracks.
Shall we go there and experience them?
Or should they remain a mystery
Whose attributes we can assign through our minds?
As we return to the lake,
Dust rises from our footsteps,
We cross a small stream racing downward,
We stop and think of past small rivulets
We have encountered,
And how all give us some unstated longing.
Are they longings of loss
Of remembrance of their beauty?
Are they longing for other small stream crossings?
Will we ever be satisfied by enough
Lakes, mountains and streams?
Will we ever feel enough wilderness?
Will we ever be satisfied?
Will we ever savor enough
Of the world in reality or in our minds

SEVEN POEMS ON LOVE

THE BEGINNING OF A ROMANCE

On a hot spring day
In the shade
A chance encounter
Both seeking relief
From the sun's rays

The beginning of a romance
Continuing after these many years
Our love now growing deeper
With each passing year

How our lives are set forever
By such chance encounters

LOVE DESPAIR

To take love for life is an oversight
Yet love does lead us to despair
As always when thinking hazy thoughts at night
Why does love lead to disrepair?

We met while walking along the lake path
She passing asked the path direction
I said it was a never ending path
To love of great infinite discretion

We became lovers, but it did not last
Was I to blame for its failure?
Or was it meant to become a love past?
Could we have stopped love failure?

So even great love can lead to despair
So painful yet can we seek love repair?

LOVE LOST

Nearby hills dark with eucalyptus cover
Reflected on the lake nearby
Swans floating high, cormorants low in water
Or airing wings on shore close-by

Walking the shore chasing birds from perches
I think of love not long ago
Near this lake we often met for lunches
With talks of our lives not long ago

Our eyes met with smiles while I was speaking
I could not stop looking at her
Erotic dreams would leave me always burning
With desire as she would confer

Great age difference turned me away
Fools indeed are we who let such hold sway

PARADISE SOUGHT

I remember the long walk to paradise
Set upon a trail of granite
The walk was taken with little advice
From lover or other invite

Was paradise achieved without disgrace?
Was paradise worth the long walk?
Was paradise what I wished to embrace?
Was paradise there only talk?

Perhaps only love is true paradise
And found at home in ones true love
Yet we humans do seek distant paradise
Although we return to our love

The human condition is sometimes strange
But what is life without a path thus strange.

MAGICAL PLACES

Will you walk with me to magical places
In the mountains and in my mind?
Let us think my adored of deep blue lakes,
Shining in sunlight of the mind

Do you as I think with rapture of love
As the lake turns ominous with clouds?
We hold each other tight expressing love
Marveling at the closing shroud

As sun sets, mountain spires are mirrored
Does your spirit soar to spires,
Although you to the ground are now rooted?
Does your mind explore the spires?

In spires a mind explores new ideas
Which adds puzzles to one's life ideals.

INEXPLICABLE LOVE

My love has oft rejected my advance
We oft speak to each other with pleasure
And we each other with pleasure enhance
And she is still my life desire

What does she in me expect and desire?
What do I wish today of her?
Will ever the two of us yet conspire?
Will we be apart forever?

Mystery of love precludes an answer
An age old fate of many loves
And forever stay the lonely dancer
For this the fate for many loves

That which life has thrust upon humankind
Is inexplicable in love we find

SEXES

I look on the scene of lake romantic
Which gives some thoughts of past loves lost
Who caused loss, he or she, though romantic?
Did he or she poor argue most?

Will ever the sexes communicate?
Or are they forever held apart?
Will their equal pride preclude conciliate?
Or will neither attempt a start?

What wishes do we all surely desire?
Can love and thought make compassion?
Is conversation what we do aspire
To bring both conciliation?

An age old quandary of love and life
Not solved still a thing of human strife.

VOYAGES

A NEW WORLD VOYAGE

THE PEOPLE SPEAK

Silence from the grave,
Silence from the dead,
And the poor man said:
In the days when the world was flat
There was nothing but a rat,
When the world became round
The new world was found
And the rat was displaced by a cat.

An act of the brave,
Words from the coward
And the rich and the poor put forward:
In all of the days of the past
There has always been time for a fast ,
But time for dreams is something it seems
That never has elapsed.

COMMENTARY

Since the rich and the poor have agreed
It is time for a new world of greed
A voyage should start to an unknown part
To see if it's sound that the world is round.

THE VOYAGE

Should we sail to the left or the right?
Now that depends on the worded fright,
And even though it is seldom night
We'll never sail when the sun is bright:
Our ship is of lead and the sea is not dead
And the wakes at night are iridescently bright.
The storms out at sea would be easy to take
Could only we find the right word at stake
But the trouble as always is an overcast haze
That leaves one and all in a variable daze.

THE FIRST LAND OF CALL

The first land of call was a place where all fall,
And while greed was quite great
Most was left up to fate,
An interesting place for the lazy or hazy,
But both rich and poor were after much more.
Then we sank off shore and talked to a whore.

THE UNDERSEA WHORE TALKS

"In our land of the deep
The prices are steep,
And the coffers are filled
By those never stilled:
We'll float your ship
If the price is nice
And with the grand tradition of our clan
We'll send you off with our smiles and wiles."

THE VOYAGE CONTINUES
AND A PIRATE INTERLUDE

We raised our ship and sailed away
After the whore received her pay;
We were soon waylaid by a pirate who said:
"Though your ship is of lead
From a short distance
For a long instance---
Your ship was of silver and gold,
Shimmering in the moonlight
And looked as Eldorado to the Spanish might--
Our disappointment's great,
Enough to make us hate---
But our greed is so great
We must make a new date
With a ship that's true,
And a crew that's new
And true blue".

COMMENTARY

The rich and the poor were at first elated,
Since the pirate in so many words stated
That greed could be greater than hate,
But that was the crescent
And all that were present
Crossed and re-crossed,
Began anew, and rehearsed
Where in the world is nothing cursed.

THE VOYAGE CONTINUES

We sailed along without a care,
And almost failed to pay our fare,
The mate thought we were sinking,
But that didn't stop the drinking,
And the wind that blew,
Kept the course true,
As we revolved about a circle.

WE MEET A MAN OF THE WORLD

A gale came up and all became stormy,
The day all dark and gloomy,
Then a wave broke over the bow,
And brought with it a man,
Who spoke with command:
"I am a lawyer bold,
And have always been one to hold;
A peril out at sea,
Or wherever you may be,
Whether by your hand or not,
Is something to be bought,
So cross my palms and place yourself
In the hands of my fate".

COMMENTARY

The equality of all
Is not about to fall
As long as everything is one and all,
And the same are all and one.

THE VOYAGE CONTINUES

Days became seas,
Land became time,
And all we found was a nursery rhyme
Of where else we stopped much could be said,
But we leave that to the thoughts of the dead,
For all was the same,
Yet nothing was tame,
And the greed was the same as before,
The same sort of thing as the whore
(Although the occupations were more)

THE RETURN

The voyage lasted an eon,
And the lights became those of neon,
But as Columbus found,
The world is quite round, and greed is as great,
But not greater;
So rich and poor returned,
Scuttled their ship and turned,
Their backs to the looking glass,
And lived their lives as a case of hives,
And never got one bit better.

SUMMATION

Silence from the grave,
Silence from the dead,

An act of the brave,
Words from the coward,
And all put forward:
The world which we cherish,
If we aren't to perish,
Is as rich as the rest,
And as poor as the best.

RETURN OF THE FLAT WORLD

PROLOGUE

Can it be that after all
We have now returned to a flat world?
To find out we started a new voyage,
Hoping not to fall off the edge of the world,
And seeking to discover a new world order.

We set sail and it started to hail,
Shredding our billowing sails,
With this inauspicious start,
We boldly set a straight course
To the end of the world.
We soon encountered another ship
And was greeted by its Captain,

THE CAPTAIN SPEAKS

"Don't travel in such a straight line,
You are bound to be distracted from your time
By Sirens galore."

We laughed at the Captain's warning,
But were soon hearing a sound so pretty,
That we took pity and sailed directly to it.

THE SIRENS SING

"Of what can you be thinking,

To believe that the world is round,
And created by random forces,
That's not a solution,
For a deity in seven days did the world create,
With all the creatures in their place,
What folly of rocks wearing down and filling seas,
Yet later to be raised to heights above.
Were that true, where is the religious magic?"

INTERLUDE

With effort, we escaped the Sirens and sailed on,
Eager to hail the end of the world,
If it, indeed, exists.

We crept along the endless ocean,
Without undo emotion,
Until an Evangelist approached our ship,
with evangelical emotion.

THE EVANGELIST AND HIS SERMON

"O faithless ones,
You are but lost without the
Lord singing righteousness.
Sing now fervently of tragedy of dead fetuses,
Killed by humanists in the face of natural order.
A fiery Hell is surely your fate,
Unless you repent
And raise your voices in songs of the righteous,
And return to God".

INTERLUDE

While taken back by the Sirens and the Evangelist,
We sailed on and on in a straight direction.
After endless days without a list,
We became becalmed,
But then a politician approached our ship
And spoke both assertively,
And in a lively manner.

THE POLITICIAN ORATES

"You have been hearing the voices of the masses,
Expressed through Sirens and Evangelist.
I have heard them and they bring votes,
So I say the world is flat and full of crap,
But I love those votes,
So why not bring love to all with a flat world."

THE VOYAGE CONTINUES

We sailed on and on and never
Found the end of the world,
But, rather, circumnavigated the Earth
And ended back where we started.

SUMMATION

In the beginning all thought the world flat,
And it was not sound that the world was round,
And we were the center of the universe
We discovered, in spite of opposition of the church,

Through Galileo and Columbus
That the earth is round and revolves around our sun
And the sun is but infinitesimal in the universe,
Thus, the center of the universe is very far away.

We have been placid in our knowledge
Of the evolution of man
Of all that has been learned
Over centuries of striving
Through contributions
Of scientists and philosophers
Now we are challenged by those
Who would return us to Devine Creation,
And ignore our evolution.

The continuing application of such thinking
Will return us to the past.
Why not, then, return to a flat world?
If free thought can be suppressed,
The return to medieval thinking
Will lead us to a medieval way of life,
Dominated by despots and clergy,
And the world will be flat.

CONTRAILS

A jet airplane appearing on the horizon, travels
across the sky, to the opposite horizon,
With its sound traveling well behind it,

When the upper atmosphere is dry,
The contrail is small and travels
Tightly behind the jet and
Upon reaching the far horizon
Both disappear into nothingness.

When the upper atmosphere is wet
The contrails may form clouds
Which dissipate very slowly
And may grow for some time,
Before finally disappearing,
Leaving behind a temporary essence of the aircraft.

A modern jet may handle three hundred people.
But are there people on the airplane?
And what is the evidence of their existence?

Regardless of a dry or wet upper atmosphere
What happens to their essence when the jet passes
Beyond the horizon?

Is this like life it self?
What essence does a person leave upon death?
Perhaps a remembrance in the minds
Of spouse, children and friends

But they too will exit the Earth some day,
Then the only essence left
May be faded photographs
Disappearing all too quickly.

Very few of us will ever do things
Remembered for long by anyone.
Yet, perhaps, to simply strive in our
Lives is sufficient.

DREAMS OF LIFE

Life is but a set of dreams
We all play out
Though out our passage

Past loves ephemeral
Yet remembered
Or was it only one dream?

Although felt
Adventures come and go
What remains of them?

My children, now adults
Remembered as children
Where has their youth gone?

My youth
Remembered clearly
And yet is gone

My parents
I see as active adults
They are now long dead

The transient nature
Of everything
Is everywhere evident

All we can do
Is live and dream
Day by day.

THE PIONEER

The pioneer with his wife so dear,
Crossed the plains in a horse drawn carriage,
To till with his hands the far off lands.

With the guise of a man that's wise,
He fought the Indians and the drought,
For a home where the deserts roam.

Though the plains are still dry what a far cry,
From the motorist now who hasn't a plow,
Who drives all the way in a couple of days.

And with the guise of a man that's wise,
Fights the traffic that's quite terrific,
For a swimming pool he hopes will be cool.

THE TORTUOUS PATH

Throughout our lives we follow a tortuous path
Containing waysides of measured decisions
 - and snap ones,
And waysides of loves lost and gained,
And of jobs not taken and ones taken, good or bad.
Of Universities attended and those rejected.
Of majors considered, but not taken
And those taken by mere chance.

Of friends acquired and later lost.
Of places lived in and loved but abandoned.
Of places visited and retained in our minds,
Sometimes later revisited,
Or sometimes never again visited.

Waysides of chance encounters,
Some resulting in long term friends
Some forgotten the next day.

Of visits to other continents and countries
All changing our views on life and our world.
Of friends made overseas, some still contacted
 - from time to time.

All the world found along the tortuous,
Uncertain path
Often not planned, oft disappointing
Sometimes rough, but marvelous in its entirety.

TWENTY FIVE RAMBLINGS

#1

Wind blowing in the pines,
Where is the water I hear?
Can the wind send water?
Or must I find it myself?

#2

Grow, grow little one.
As I grew once
See where growing got me
If I had really grown where would I be?

#3

Outward looks catch
Glances back
Seeing sometimes
Or so it seems
What was not to be seen.

#4

How do you put together
What you want?
When I can't put together
What I have to do.

#5

I look up to the mountain
Hoping to see high places
I may see them
But, do I ever reach them?

#6

When looking down a road,
Its fun to think of where it leads,
And of all the people near it.
Do they, too, look down the road,
And think of where it leads,
And of all the people near it?

#7

Wandering by a library stack,
Wondering what each book contains,
What will I miss?
What will I never see or think?
Because my mind discarded,
And my hand never moved.

#8

When can I,
Who is bound here,
Rise, too?

Why do I,
Who can think,
Not rise?

Why must only they,
Who believe in that which is superficial
Seem certain?

What is there in idols,
That keeps men certain,
Even idols without moral force?

#9

Near where I live is a beautiful church,
Beautiful in a classic manner and ivy covered,
The ivy twines its way into one's soul,
Now is this soul the soul to be saved?
From what should the soul be saved?
Unless it could be from the ugly,
Which is to be found inside,
This church with the beautiful façade.

#10

Lightly I sparkle,
Like a Roman candle,
For I am of my time and country,
Like the Romans before us,
And like the Romans before us,
We shall one day be no more.

#11

How high are the mountains?
Can we ever measure them?
And if we can,
Should we want to?
Is not their existence enough?

#12

Will you climb higher with me,
Into the clouds,
Where the wind blows and it is always damp,
If you follow me even higher,
There is a place above the clouds,
Where the sun always shines,
And sometimes the wind doesn't blow.

#13

Cares are here and vanish,
And covered in time by varnish,
Then who can remember?
A thought arrives,
And sees,
And then forever,
Is lost.

#14

Towns are bright,
Towns are light,
Laughter is bright,

Stars are bright,
Time is light,
Time is bright,
Man is light,
But is he bright?

#15

To a house of mystery and toil,
A mastery of magic,
By a person near tragic.

#16

A grand finale of love,
For a place that's wooden,
With a care and a shove.

#17

Passion eager,
Work forever,
And never, never,
Leave her.

#18

An empty victory of the heart,
And somewhere in the dark,
A black light of hope and despair.

#19

An effort wasted and of wood,
Showers of sparks and ashes,
For what has she stood?

#20

Inanimate men,
For all their thunder,
Arrive with blunder,
To what end?

#21

Beauty is a thing illusive,
So rare and yet so common,
Something we can never summon,
A thing we can not touch, but must,
An apparition we must be near,
But hopeless to hold dear,
For beauty lives and beauty fades.

#22

Stars shine down on all terrain
Mountains, prairies, cities, wilderness
Or did at one time
Before the city lights blotted them out
Or decreased their brilliance.

#23

Between twilight and dawn lies night
In the arctic winter there may be no light
Yet in mid summer there is only day
Unless clouds make everything grey

#24

Is our age one of constant strife?
Without hope for compassion
What is the reason for such life?
Can we not have a finer mission?

#25

Scenes of joy and devastation,
Interplay many times after creation.
Is the interplay random?
Are we manipulated with abandon?

CITIES

PROGRESS

Laughter in the streets,
Cracked plaster in the houses,
Yesterday nothing,
Today everything's new and shining,
All in a city born of ideas,
People talk with smiles of children and the future,
All are very young and radiate
With laughter and none hesitate,
See my new Ford,
How can one be bored?
Seventy five an hour
And I'm next in line for promotion.
See the smoke from the new factory:
That's muscles for the land and money.
Let's take a ride into the country,
See that billboard,
It's not pasteboard,
It's real progress.
We're a city,
Everything's pretty,
And in such a few years,
Why, there's no room for tears
Come be happy,
Don't think of the ruts and be unhappy,
Kiss and make up.
That house over there,
Up in a day, not in a year,
And when it blows down in ten years,
You say tears?

No! No!
More work more seventy five,
And a new house.
Listen to that motor purr,
Not a noise and we're going ninety five.
Too fast?
Speed is good and clean.
Oh, here's our new house,
Listen to the factory noise,
You couldn't hear a mouse.
See the modern furniture,
And as a result of architecture
You can't even see the crack.
You don't like the style?
It's the very latest style.
You must need help.
Where's that psychiatrist's number?
Anyway, he's a real comer.
Why my sister had a breakdown,
And he cured her for nothing down

A FACTORY OF MEN

A steel and concrete dome of the city,
A factory of men,
Who are shaped by everything but pity,

They sweat and toil and never cry,
Of accomplishments there are many,
Of gains, not any,

And into the night more work,
No rest, no thought,
And they find naught,

Sleep is but a break until tomorrow,
And what is the stake?

A place in the City,
With no pity,
And even accomplishments,
Bear fruit for none,

Yet what is, must be done,
And who can fight the mighty?

There's all but pity,
And thought and feeling,
And time will not stop,

When steel is heart,
And cement is pity,

And love is City,

And a factory of men,
Is but pity,
And a place of the City.

A DISASTER IN NEW ORLEANS AND MISSISSIPPI

Levies failing, water rising, bodies floating,
Houses crushed
Poor blacks with nothing grieving,
With loved ones lost
Eyes dazed, soldiers helping, sometimes threatening
People fleeing, sometimes clinging to a house
Wading, riding in a boat
A ruined city, a devastated coast

Americans eager to help victims,
Open hearts, open wallets, willing help.

Images of another America
Poor as in the poorest of places
Often black
Where is the great American dream?
Is this a scene from rich America?
Shacks, homeless, crime,
Little health care, few services,
Third world America, why here?

A LAND APART

PROLOGUE

Where is there a land where things are grand,
And people seldom complain of their Kingdom?

THE LAND

Let the people of this land,
Individually state their passions and beliefs.

A WORKER SPEAKS

"I work in a factory of steel,
And go to work with zeal.
After my shift I go home to my wife,
Via a pub I also call home."

THE BAR MAID

"Those slovenly men who come to my bar,
Make passes after too many glasses,
But the pay and the tips are good,
So what more could one ask for?"

THE WORKER'S WIFE

"My husband comes home with tainted breath,
Slaps me and the children,
And sits downs to dinner in a silent manner,

Ignoring our children and me,
He grunts through dinner
And retires to a football game."

THE WORKER'S BOSS

"People working in my shop,
Are all members of our Union,
And work as little as they can,
But they do produce a top notch product."

THE MINISTER

"My work place is that of God,
I lead my flock as they wish,
I often see right from wrong,
And sometimes that is what the congregation wants,
But often I must compromise to maintain
The Church's edifice.
So all is harmony and light in my house of God."

THE ELECTED POLITICIAN

"I represent the people as they wish to be represented,
Of course, allowing for extra rewards
From those with money
Who wish special things done, so I line my pockets,
But they probably are good things for the people.
And they will thank me in the long run."

THE ENGINEER

"The design of an industrial plant
Requires, skill, imagination, knowledge
And care for the environment.
There is little room for compromise,
But there always must be compromise.
What is the answer?
Should we cheat?
Is that the answer?

A well run factory has splendid beauty,
But will it meet cost expectations?
Will no one notice when we cut quality?
Or safety?"

THE PHYSIAN

"House calls are a thing of the past,
But with proper insurance you can prosper,
As can I and all the health care workers,
And especially the industrial manufacturers,
Of drugs and anti-biotics.
No Insurance? Then surely you have not worked,
And deserve nothing."

THE PATRIOT

"Of course our land is the best and most bountiful,
Come wave the flag and support our troops,
For they fight for our oil and our independence,

All on the other side of the world,
And is not God on our side?"

THE MAYOR

"I am the mayor of the greatest city,
We grow at a rate not pretty.
So the fields vanish and become asphalt,
But growth is always the way of prosperity.
And who wants poverty?"

THE AUTOMOBILE CEO

"We build beautiful automobiles for the masses.
They simply love the SUV,
And the bigger the better.
So what if requires a war to fuel this monster,
The war is certainly well worth it.
Even a holy war with men of bombs."

THE UNIVERSITY STUDENT

"I attend my classes on time,
And do my homework on time.
Assignments are straight forward.
My grades have improved since I started cheating.
I'm certain now to be admitted to medical school.
Cheating is dangerous, but if you don't,
You are unfit for medical school,
And unfit to be a medical doctor."

THE UNIVERSITY PROFESSOR

"My students are mediocre,
But expect respect and loyalty,
Although they do not expect to give it.
I pass them on and look for good evaluations.
My research is mediocre,
But I give granting agencies what they want,
And am not wanting for research funds.
I hope soon to be a full Professor."

THE PEOPLE

"We the people are proud of our land,
We can destroy whatever we can
While waving our flag on a motor bike or an ATV.
How wonderful it is to see our tracks
And beer can leavings
What a great land where
We are all so free and think not of the future"

MEANNESS AND THE CITY

The frantic pace accelerates
As population shifts advance
And from desert vistas cities appear,
Blotting out the vistas.

As the cities grow, the traffic becomes horrific,
The civility decreases and the meanness increases,
Tough laws are implemented,
But do these also increase the meanness?

Children are herded, monitored
And controlled in a strict environment.
How will children be able to achieve,
Freedom in this mean, suppressed environment?

NEWCASTLE, AUSTRALIA

Newcastle, once with steel works
Now a seaside resort with surfing
At the base of the Hunter Valley
Where coal competes with wine making
Near a rain forest with aerial ferns
And snow gums atop high points
Where often mists are forming.

Newcastle now so benign though once
A place where prisoners worked a sawmill
And bushrangers terrorized all
But now a place for bathers at once
Playing in ocean pools next to a hill
And thinking of wine tours beyond that hill

Yet even now the large coal carriers,
Oft three dozen in number
Stand off shore waiting to come into port
To pick up a cargo of coal
For Newcastle remains the world's
Largest port shipping coal.

AMERICA'S WORKERS

Every day the pace accelerates
Driving all to frantic haste
Management reduces work force
Resulting in more work and acceleration

With threats of outsourcing
Managers give out more work
And reduce vacation time
Workers strive to keep up

Meanness envelops the land
Workers attempt advantage
By disparaging fellow workers
Those who fail to follow
Are left behind and issued pink slips

Management, if high enough
Gives themselves heft bonuses
While reducing health care
And retirement benefits for those
Unable to fight back

Can America retain its enviable place
With such behavior the norm?
Can American remain a First World Nation
And the ideal of the world?

PARQUE FARROUPILHA

Named after a failed revolution,
An insurgency of two million people
Seeking redress and a separate country
Led by passionate and bold leaders

Bento Gonçalves da Silva, Antônio de Sousa Netto,
Guiseppi Garibaldi, Anita Ribeiro Garibaldi among
The many patriots and many immigrants,
The *Açores* and the two thousand Germans
Who took part in the insurgency.

Defeated in the end by a magnanimous man,
Field Marshall Luis Alves de Lima e Silva
Who offered amnesty and reconciliation

Located in the center of *Porto Alegre*
The beautiful trees, fountains and flowers
It is a refuge from steel and concrete
And a place of rallies and displays

The flee market on Saturdays is exciting
The local painters and artists displaying wares,
Paintings, old object, clothes, flowers and antiques.

Rallies for the symphony orchestra,
And other popular and cultural events
Plus political rallies for such as the Red Party,

Having gained the *Rio Grande do Sul* state house
Displaying banners and shirts with the likeness
Of Che Guervara, still an icon to the poor

I recall many walks in the park,
Either by myself or sometimes accompanied
By a friend and her little dog,
Oft watching the many picnics and playing children
Overhead the aerial ferns and orchids
Brought an exotic feel to the walk
And as one reached a street
A reminder of the surrounding city
And its frantic pace.

POLITICS, WAR, REVOLUTION
AND HORROR

THE MEAN SOCIETY

A terrible necessity of time and place
In which to live
Amid an accelerating frantic pace
An increasingly mean society alive

Is our age one of constant strife?
Without hope for compassion
What is the reason for such life?
Can we not have a finer passion?

Must we always elect leaders with negative passion?
Who think but of personal glory
Who neglect our people
And start wars without compassion
With torture without compassion but ever gory

Why do we love our guns and not our poor?
Why do the poor love guns over health?
Why does society have such poor?
Why do we so at expense of others so love wealth?

Where are we going blindly and selfishly?
What grand scheme do we see for ourselves?
In our country where we invoke the word of God
For any and every purpose so willfully
Proclaiming we are the righteous and just.

CHE

In the end he met death
In a rainforest at the hands of troops
Paid for by a nation of wealth
He lived for ideals of a society never proven
Yet he today still is an icon of hope
For millions of people his ideals proven.

Who was he of such devotion to a cause unproven?
Why is his likeness displayed at rallies?
And at scenes of protest of the masses.
And is revered throughout the downtrodden.
Yet after Cuba his efforts were all for naught
And in the end his death was bought
By leaders of a nation violent.

His followers were adoring and reverent
He was trained as a medical healer
Yet he chose to pursue a path different
Unless he thought through the violence
Of his revolutions he was, indeed, a healer
Of injustice and poverty brought by foreign
Nations of selfish violence.

Were his efforts and sacrifice in vain?
But can this be to have such passion in followers
After all these years since his death in vain.
Surely somewhere justice and good for followers
Must prevail and freedom realized.
Yet there is no guarantee for righteousness realized

He was a man of the favored and elite
Yet through observation of poverty and passion
He dedicated himself to a cause of compassion.
Will the future forever continue poverty of masses?
Was his striving in vain
And the world yet without compassion?

But what if he had won
And the world became communist?
Would it be as he imagined or would it be fascist?
What would the world be like?
Full of compassion or a world of terror?

FALSE ACTS OF THE FREE

Why are we here?
What unconscionable acts did we commit?
Were we merely listening to our leaders?
Were the acts simply fits of patriotism?
Was it simply pride in our country?

Now we fight a war based on lies.
Now we torture and pretend we don't
Or try to justify it.

Our young men die in a far off land
Put there by visions of oil
And visions of empire by ruthless leaders.

Selling our morality and freedom, yet
Feeling good and just about it, and
Selling our freedom for perceived safety

How can it be that we sell ourselves so cheaply?
Perhaps, even, pay to lose
Our humanity in loss of freedom,
And loss in self esteem.

POLITICIANS AND THE PUBLIC

Do politicians lie about their promises,
Because that is what the public wishes?
Do they only play to the most selfish wishes
Of a few selfish people
Because that is what the public wishes?
Is the problem with politicians in reality a problem
With the populace who think not of consequences
Beyond tomorrow

What price will humans pay
For such arrogant raping and trashing?
The ultimate toll can not even be guessed.

OUR CORRUPTION

What drives us now to act the fool
And accept the progress of our nation
That accepts the most corrupt politicians
And accepts as friends nations
Of the most corrupt intensions

We fly our flag and think ourselves patriotic
When we tolerate terrible torture
At our hands and allies
We pretend reverence when we face the world
Yet what reverence is it that we hold dear?

Is it the grasp for oil and the lowest denominator?
And all nations are welcome to our fold regardless
Of their acts as long as they accept us
And only kill those we wish killed
And, if totalitarian, as long as they obey us.

Can we forever survive if we act thus?
What hope have we then?
Are we to become another third world nation
And subjugated by those we now scorn?
What is the answer to our dilemma?

OUR TIMES

A terrible time in which to live and think
Our ruthless leaders send us to endless war
We bombed a nation and killed far more
Than the despot we replaced
We torture and deny it
- Or try to justify it
On the flimsiest of grounds
All for goals of oil and Empire

The war has now turned Holy
And our enemies disintegrate themselves
If they can but destroy some of us
With the words "Praise God" on their lips
And with visions of a Martyr's Paradise

Can we hope to win this Holy war?
And not lose our humanity.

FLAG WAVING

It does not matter what political system
We enjoy—or hate
For political leaders to lead us into
Unconscious acts of hatred and suppression
Is simply to create fear of the unknown enemy
And to wave the flag with cries of patriotism.

TOM DOOLEY AND JOHN KENNEDY

Tom Dooley was a man of compassion
He went to Vietnam to aid poor people
Receive medical treatment
He started hospitals
And got medicines delivered

His compassion overflowed to rescuing
Beleaguered churches and their pastors
Threatened by the North Vietnam Communists

He wrote a book *Deliver Us from Evil*
Detailing torture treatment of Catholic Priests
And children by the Communist Rulers,
- later shown fictitious

He advocated transfer of Vietnamese Catholics
From the North to the then free South
He died soon after starting this movement
Which was taken up by President Kennedy,
A man of power and aggression

And looking for reasons to invade the country
Since he felt our interests threatened
In South East Asia
And sent troops to Vietnam
He then, too, died
Within two years

Tom Dooley and John Kennedy
Hang down your heads in shame
And cry - for all those who were soon to die.

THE EVENTS LEADING TO THE PRESENT

What has led us to our present state?
Must we start at mid twentieth century?
What are the events that have shaped us?
Did it start with our nuclear aggression in Japan?
Followed by the Korean war
And our defense of Berlin

Were these things good or bad?
And these are but distant events
Although they affect us today

We cannot take all credit for today
For the Chinese Great leap forward still affects us
As does the earlier Bolshevik Revolution
And many other great and tragic events of the
Past one hundred years

Our Presidents are aggressive men
So when confronted with
International strife
React with aggression and often
Terrible things start
With the greatest of intentions

In Vietnam Dr. Tom Dooley
With his religion on his sleeve
Convinced our reigning President

That North Vietnam religious suppression
Must be stopped from entering
The South of the country
Never again was a cry

With these great intensions
President Kennedy sent our troops into
South Vietnam and a loss of innocence

SHIPWRECKED ON A FOREIGN SHORE

The voyage begin with gusto
With cheers from those on board
 - and those on shore
Amid flag waving and strong oratory

We sailed ahead with confidence
Shattering all obstacles in our path
Leaving only ruins in our wake
Storms may have raged
But we ignored them with
Knowledge that we were invincible

We reasoned that God was with us
With our righteousness
We were arrogant in the course we set
How were we to know
 - of hidden turbulence
 - of hidden mines
 - of other's righteousness

Our thundering crash onto the forbidden shore
Surprised us and shook us
Our values were called in question
As was our reasoning

Yet we could not leave that awful shore
And became mired there

Our people there were harassed,
 And sometimes died

What was this voyage about?
What did we get from it?
Except what should be humility
But is a deep questioning
Of the course our Capitan
And his mates forced upon us.

THE AMERICAN CIVIL WAR

Terrible wars are fought for many reasons
For empire, expansion, religion, and hate
All are stupid but coveted by nations
Men hurl themselves to death in battle
Behind a flag in terror with manliness

Are any of them worth cruel death in battle?
And will men's death mark them nation saviors?
Do leaders sacrifice men for nation's gain?
Or do they arrogantly discard them?
For their own ambitious leadership

The worst of wars are fought between brothers
As was the great American Civil War
North against South over a terrible practice
Of slavery of people of color
Yet men fought to the death to retain it

The war took a toll on American lives
And who was to blame for starting the war?
And who was responsible for its length?
Could it have been stopped once it began?
Where had good minds gone terribly awry?

Did the Southerners firing on Sumpter
Have any idea what hell they had started?
And the deaths that were to come North and South
The war started with a minor event
But soon grew to horrendous proportions

Abraham Lincoln the emancipator
Could he have ended slavery with out
Terrible carnage South and North alike?
Could Robert E Lee great Southern General
Been more universal and less provincial?
Could Confederate hot heads have had less pride?

There were horrible images through the war
The lake of blood at Shiloh spilled by men
The corn field at Antietim with only dead
Pickett's Confederate charge at Gettysburg
The scorched earth march of Sherman to the sea

To view the carnage at Shiloh should have
Convinced anyone of the war's futility
For casualties were equal to Waterloo
And twenty more battles of equal magnitude
Were yet to come before war's bloody end

All this for the right to keep men enslaved
Yet very few were those who would do better
Sam Houston tried but failed to keep Texas Union
And spoke of the war's futility for the South
None other tried at all and many died in pain

Confederate soldiers oft risked maiming
And horrible death believing they were
Defending their birth land from invaders
Union soldiers often idealistic
Risked life to keep the Union intact

The war wore on and Robert E. Lee fought
Bloody battle after battle until
His troops could move no more ending the war
Ulysses S. Grant sacrificed man after man
To bring the bloody end at Appomattox

Stonewall Jackson brilliant in a battle
Out witting the Yankees in every conflict
Viciously cutting them down as they ran
A God fearing demonic destroyer
For him God's work was done when soldiers died

Cruel Sherman and his scorched earth policy
Showed future despots and democracies
A way to attack an enemy through vicious
Attack on non combatants and innocents
A truly detestable legacy

To name a few of the many battles
Manasas, Shiloh, Antietim, Vicksburg
Wilderness, Gettysburg, Cedar Creek, Westport,
Chickamauga, Chancellorsville, Corinth,
New Madrid, Utoy Creek, many others

Jefferson Davis much maligned President
And Commander of the Confederacy
Could not hold Confederate States together
Saw the Confederacy fall apart
But could not stop the terrible slaughter

*Mine eyes have seen the power and the glory
Of the Lord*, a song designed to send men

Into ruinous battle and martyrdom
A Christian call to painful cruel death
What more evil song has ever been written?

Men dying in agony and deformed
Without let up for four devastating
Years in battle and in hospital beds
Some for freeing slaves and some to keep slaves
Had no one any sense or human purpose?

Southern soldiers fought to keep slaves yet
Very few owned them nor would they ever do so
Yet they died for the few rich who owned them
And to keep the slavery economy
And humans bound to others and hopeless

After Gettysburg the South was beaten
Further fighting was useless but bloody
Yet none could stop continuing slaughter
And the war dragged on for two more years
Two more years of shame North and South alike

For all the horror of the many battles
More men died the true soldier's death in bed
Not by that of the violent Red Horse
But by that of the exhausting Pale Horse
Can not men ever do better than deadly War?

After the war was freedom for blacks realized
True freedom was thwarted by Klu Klux Klan
And harsh separation of the races
Blacks in the South remained in servitude
In the fields and in positions menial

It took many decades before real freedom
It took a great leader's non-violent pleas
And the oratory of Martin Luther King
And a brave woman on a segregated bus
To make beginning inroads on freedom

Where are we today in our great nation?
Is true equality realized yet?
A look at our nation shows that great strides
Must still be realized before completeness
Of equality is to be achieved

The Civil War, an unsettling example
Of the horror of war and futility
And how war affects nations and peoples
Always in a great negative manner
For depressing decade after decade

By contrast slaves were freed in Brazil without
Undo strife and rancor in manner peaceful
Now race relations in Brazil are better
And now less discrimination exists
All the races coexist in quiet harmony.

DICK CHENEY

Dick Cheney, the man with the perpetual snarl
In the corner of his mouth
Failed to follow a cardinal rule of the NRA
On a hunting trip
 - to know where fellow hunters are at all times.
Neglecting this he heard a movement behind him
Thinking it a quail he turned
And blasted a fellow hunter.
Or was he annoyed by this man?

Police were not notified for some hours.
Did Dick Cheney and his cohorts think
Of suppressing the shooting?
But were discovered? What were they up to?

What will the President do?
Can he ask Dick Cheney to resign?
But then he would not have Cheney's
Advice on foreign and domestic affairs.

BOMBING INNOCENTS

A killer nation bombing
At the slightest provocation
Bomba, bomba, bomba
Random destruction
Although specific targets are sought

Civilians, children are not spared
Our enemy says there are no innocents
And this we must believe
Since before attacking we always bomb
Bomba, bomba, bomba

Our history is one of violence
And now we are more effective
At killing and maiming

Can this violence be reversed?
Can we even reverse violence?
Committed on our own.
Have we no compassion?

THE VORTEX

As we swirl about in our daily lives
We attempt to keep ourselves out of the maelstrom
Between Scylla and Charybdis,
From which escape is impossible
Where sirens beckoning will surely lead us
To our destruction.

One's must always guard against
Classical temptations of
Pride, greed, anger, avarice,
Lust, sloth, gluttony
But what about
Pride, greed and lust, avarice
Of our lying leaders
Which can be seductive.

THE CRISIS

Day in and day out
A crisis of the day or week
How else can a Government function?
- or a business

If not existing then created
For a crisis allows action with out thought
Eliminating rational thinking
A good panic can move peoples
To do anything a Government
- or a business wishes

Thus, bad Government or business
- protects itself

What will be the crises for this week?
Terrorism or the economy

RELIGION, POLITICS AND HATE

DIVINE DIECTION

Divine direction, divine guidance,
A new cry from those who question evolution.
But what do these mean?
How do they fit with the natural order of life?

Is everything directed by God?
Does this mean everything given man
By divine direction
Is in harmony with the world order?
He obviously has been given a brain.
And can think on his own.
What can man do, thus, on his own?
Can he build cities?
Can he cut down forests?
Can he do all that he has done over the past?
He has done all these things.

Can he clone embryos?
He has done so.
Is this not using what God has given him?
What are the limits of his God given gifts?
Why can't he clone humans?

Is not to deny this, limiting his God given gifts?
Are, then, those who prevent such use of gifts
The anti-Gods?
Are they not the Barbarians?

THE CHURCH AND COMMUNISM

Once, I visited a Turin University
After a conference at Lago Magiore,
To visit and talk to colleagues at the University
The visit was for three days
And I was wined, dined and stuffed.

An Italian colleague
Went to retrieve a daughter
At a Catholic Youth Rally
During the second day of my visit
I accompanied her
And as we arrived a local mountain climber
Was in an inspirational manner
Touting in a reverent manner
The link between vigorous,
Inspirational mountaineering
And Catholicism
At the end of the rally
Dozens of balloons were released
In a spectacle grand.

After my visit,
And in the early evening not wishing a large meal
I strolled along the upper Po
Watching rowers in sculls test their strength,
Twos, Fours and Eights
When I came upon a communist rally
With communist banners displayed
And with the International played

I strolled in it out of curiosity.
I spotted a stand where hamburgers were sold.
I jumped for joy,
For such was just the simple meal I sought
Before long there appeared
Another local mountain climber
Who begin with ardor extolling,
The virtues of climbing to communist ideals
At the end of festivities,
Dozens of balloons were sent aloft.
It appears that the Church
And Communism are identical in their trappings.
Those who no longer believe still must
Have the discipline of a structured society.
Does this mean that communism
Is simply another form of God?

MAN AND HEAVEN

The sea is but a bath of dreams,
The air is only atmosphere,
And whatever either of these seems,
A spade's a spade so they say,
And whoever is so sentimental
To say a spade's a club,
Is quite incidental.

To take life for life is quite alright,
To take life for love,
Is very much an oversight,
A man's a man, a thing's a thing,
And they who like to say,
Man is something more than man,
I say to them, nay.

To dedicate one's life for life is
Doing things correctly,
To dedicate one's life for God,
Is something of a folly.
A man is here and God is not,
And those who for life take God,
Do little else but sit and hate

To live the present is the utmost,
To live the future,
Is as a distant outpost,
And if the present you resist,
For a place in heaven,

What assurance do you have,
That heaven's even heaven?

What hell there is,
Is what we create now,
When we could create heaven.

CHISTMAS IN THE SOUTHERN HEMISPHERE

From my apartment
Looking across the street
Hanging from apartment balconies were Santas
Wearing red winter coats of red with
Warming white ruffles

The temperature outside
Approaching 96 degrees Fahrenheit
And humidity near saturation
On the street below people
Wearing short trousers and floppies

Nearby streets decorated with Christmas lights
Shining and trees in the parks and malls
Glowing with Christmas ornaments and lights
And nativity scenes at the Cathedral
Representing Wise men and Christ's birth

At the lab Christmas party earlier
Outside the lab next to an open building
Sweltering with Christmas gifts
No hot toddies but several kegs of beer for revelers
Drinking cold liquids and finding shade
The temperature almost 100 degrees Fahrenheit

Since Christ's actual birth date is unknown
Wouldn't it make sense to declare
His birthday to be the 25th of June
In the Southern Hemisphere.

THE APOCALYPSE

The Revelations of John,
Apocalypse and the Book of the Seven Seals
An imaginable horror
Thrust upon Christians and the world
Why was it written unless to threaten
And keep control on Christians

It places martyrdom as the ultimate goal
And even necessary event of Christians
What can this hate be of world use?
Why have it part of the Christian Bible?
And why is this abomination part of a Holy book?

Yet this mean tome has been the subject
Of major musical compositions
And works of art.
What is it about the Revelations of John
That enlivens the creative muse?

JOY AND DEVASTATION

Scenes of joy and devastation,
Interplay many times after creation.
Is the interplay random?
Are we manipulated with abandon?

How to explain the successes
Followed by devastation?
How to understand the scheme of things?
Was this all planed and do we have
No say in the plan of divine intervention.
But, is this intervention devine?

ately and Jones[2,3]"

LIVING AND THINKING

THE FOREST PATH

Come along the forest path with me,
My fascinating kitten,
And I will show you the place,
Where the fog hangs low, blanketing the trail,
Where all is coolness and quiet,
And the snags are hidden.

Feel the eyes that watch, though hidden,
As we walk through the fog.
Feel how cold it is.
Are you cold?

I feel your muscles tense,
As if to spring,
Am I the prey?
Or do you want to see more.

See the branches of the forest trees,
Appearing naked through the fog,
What are you drawn to?
Why do you cling so?
Why do you tremble?

I can show you warmth,
Further up along the trail,
Where it climbs to the sun,
Why do you linger in the fog?

Run, run into the light,
Where the bright is right,
Where fangs become teeth.

Why do you stand there smiling?
Why do you keep purring?
Why don't you stop clinging?
Why don't you let go and run,
Up the trail and to the sun?

I see here only darkness,
And the night feeders,
I have no hope,
And I can't move,
And day remains forever night.

THE CIRCLE

A circular devil,
Then nothing is level.
Day becomes night,
But night is no more.

A church and its steeple
With numerous people
Start to look up, and where did they go?

Towns become cities,
Wood becomes stone,
Flesh becomes bone,
And all become none.

Two lovers are wooing,
Each other pursuing,
They started to kiss,
And love ceased to exist.

Of time there was none,
Of cries there weren't many,
Of people not any,
And all became none.

An army was marching,
The battle was nearing,
The reason was good,
Then nothing stood.

No warning, no rumble,
No shock,
And all became none.

A reason for growing
Is showing, not knowing.

Machines and machines,
And carriages and kings.

Of horses and people,
No curses, much reason.

The faster the rate,
The faster the rate,
The nearer we come
To the number one.

A horseless carriage,
A very short marriage,
No rhyme, no time,
And all became none.

The strong and the meek,
The gold and the brass,
There wasn't time for anything rash
And all there was, was past.

A horse, a house,
Where is a house?
Were there only a house,
It might not have happened,
It might not have happened.

THE LONG DISTANCE RUNNER

Although my daily run is now but a slow jog,
I once could compete well at long distance.
Yet, I still enjoy my run, be it on dirt tracks,
In the hills or on city streets.

The loneliness of the distance runner
Has been much discussed.
Yet for me the runs are always marvels of beauty,
Always inspirational, sometimes creative.
I oft see wild animals and, of course,
Myriads of plants, common local plants
Or, if abroad, exotic plants of all description
And exotic animals.
I marvel at them all.

At times while running my mind runs
At hyper speed, solving science
And mathematical problems
Or composing a poem,
Necessitating a quick trip
To a computer or notebook
To record the new poem.

Or I may think of other creative ideas,
Research papers or novels for future creation.
Or, if the thoughts are not as profound
They may be pleasant thoughts of past events
And of my family and friends.

DAY AFTER DAY

In the morning I am going to shave,
I can't see now,
The wind in the trees is overpowering,
Where are the leaves?
The steel was once blue and I hoped.
Now, every thing's red,
I am now in a forest I know,
I hate it, though I once loved it.
At one time all was blue and shinning,
And as I walked to my office in the morning,
I could hear everything,
And my heart was free.
I trusted every beam and crack,
And I always got paid.

My God greeted me every morning,
Although I never shook hands with him.
During the day the clock always
Played the same tune,
But it was merry and light.
My evenings were spent in good company,
And I never drank too much.
Maybe I never drank at all,
Perhaps I didn't drink enough,
Everything was very warm.
What now has happened to that warmth?
What brought the ice, the chill?
My bones are frozen,
My hands are brittle and cold,

My mind is ice,
I haven't smiled for a year,
And I'm blind
Hear the wind in the trees?
If only there were trees.
My beard has grown long,
But the razor, it's red,
And who can shave with rust?
Why do I take things so seriously?
The sun will still rise in the east tomorrow,
Whether anything is here or not.

When we first met there was a blue sky,
And still the sky is blue,
Why doesn't it turn red?
I don't remember purple,
There was no transition,
Only blue and then red,
And cold.

She danced out of the sky into my arms.
We shook hands,
And danced together as the leaves
And trees appeared,
Our garden grew.
There were few weeds,
And no apples.

Why is it now so bright?
I see nothing but smoke.
I can't breathe.
And as each leaf disappears,

Red appears,
And doesn't let go.

If only I could remember the path.
If only there weren't so many.
But bend, bend with the wind,
And you, too, can escape the forest without leaves,
Reach down and grasp,
And rise.

I am sailing on top of the clouds,
See there are no bounds,
No chains,
Just bend with the wind.

See her down below with the dry, dead leaves,
And the empty trees, standing
While I,
Why I soar,
Now I can shake hands,
I have no bonds,
I am shapeless.

THE GARDEN

As the clock struck the time,
Rats crept along the vine,
A myriad of emptiness came upon the stone,
The rats chewed the bone,
And left the marrow for the vultures,
Creatures appeared, hated, feasted, then were lost,
And to others played the host.

Conception, birth, life, death,
Conception, birth, life, death,
Conception, birth, life, death;
An ant, aphids, a flower, more power, cattle,
The wind, limbs and rattle,
A sunrise and shadowed figures,
Death comes and life,
And the church bells ring,
The ants with flowers in their guts,
March to their temple,
And in their manner simple,
Pray to their queen.

The rats sleep, waiting for moonlight
(Being creatures of the moon)
It can't come too soon,
They are now dead
And can't spring and seek another prey;
Midday sun, heat, dust and rust,
A whisper from the trees,
As a vulture circles, circles, circles.

Decay, I can smell decay,
Let us pray, let us pray,
I see it, I see it,
Under that tree,
We're going to be free, we're going to be free!
But spring, spring now,
And don't say how,
Tomorrow is too late,
We can't miss today's date,
And live until tomorrow,
And never, never borrow,
How then tomorrow can you spend?

Shadowed images, crawling, hiding,
None are crying,
But all are thinking,
Of tomorrow and how...
Others appear,
Some of those of the day were too late,
And met a hungry date,
But none in safety cried,
And those that died were soon night life,
And joined intimately the rats,
And if they had anything to say about it, cats.
Moonlight and site,
Of course its right,
Isn't that always so with might?

The clock struck again,
More rats on the vines,
More vines around the trees, clutching,

Holding, squeezing, hoping, praying,
And maybe winning,
But if not, to lose is to win,
Since either way the garden and its friends grow on,
Multiply, die and live on,
And end as one.

THE COLOR OF TIME

The color of the estimated
Is to be so very red,
In a tavern of blue and gold,
To see that everything will hold.

The ounces of time grow near,
In a house that's full of beer,
The human life is full of strife,
So why not try the tavern's brew?

The green mansions become very clear,
When we hold everything dear,
If we find the glass that's right,
And that is where the lights are bright.

Then drink to the lights that are so bright,
And see the day into night,
For the hour is so near,
When we lose all that's dear.

THE BLUE ROBIN

A blue robin in a red nest,
Sat on her eggs along with the best,
She hatched green chicks,
Which filled her with bliss,

Until the day came,
When her mate said "why shame,
You should be as red as your nest,
Your chicks should be as red as the rest",

At first she was filled with terror,
And thought there must be an error,
But then a second thought came to her,
"What law is there that says
A robin must always be red?"

THE SEA SHORE REMEMBERED

I long to see the sea again
Rough breakers and the rugged stacks
End of continent and of infinite ocean vistas,
Cloaking costal fog and biting coastal wind.

Ocean birds,
Both local of the nearby shores,
And from far off shores,
All noisy and fluttering,
Swooping, darting and fishing.

Nearby fishing boats,
Plying nearby banks,
And far off magic freighters,
Heading for some far off shores.
And imagined magic ports of call.

Joyous children,
Playing and striving in the sand
Building castles for destruction by their peers,
But happy after minor fights and sobs.

The admiring parents,
Sometimes snoozing and occasionally splashing,
Sometimes stealing little kisses.

The dazed magic of the time,
Swimming in our heads

Then coming to an end with a slow,
Dazed drive back home with thoughts
Of a day well spent.

FAR PLACES

I often travel to far places
And drink the essence of that land,
I marvel at the sameness with us,
Yet the differences of people there.

Although the language may be different,
Cities all have sameness,
Shopping centers are universal,
Movie theaters are universal
Streets have sameness

Houses and apartments vary,
But habitation is the same.
Yet people behave in manners different
And possess different outlooks on life
And their fellow citizens.

What is important
For each citizen of our land and theirs?
Is it freedom?
Is it health?
Are we all living on only for obliteration?
Day after day remembering things past,
And hoping for the future.

In some lands there is less hostility,
And much more civility.
There is more thought of the poor
And their rights and health and care.

Why is our nation so unkindly.
Why do we so callously
Treat the poor and unfortunate,
We who are well off,
But do not provide for those less fortunate,
Giving the excuse
That they did not earn their worth.

Will this meanness and neglect destroy us.
And lead us to hopelessness?

STRIVING

Jump back and forth across the road,
In doing so, can't you see the jumping of the toad,
As it emulates you?

We seek something that is eluding,
And can neither articulate it,
Nor come close to finding it,
On either side of the road.

What can the goal be,
When we simply jump
Back and forth across the road?
And what is the road we jump across?
Is it of our imagination?

Can you see the yellow brick pavement?
But that is but an ancient story without movement.
Is the road of dirt or bitumen?
And in what century have we commitment?

Do you see the modern jet?
Or is it merely a covered wagon?
Is the century but a concept?
And of our imagination.

We seek, but do we seek a physical place,
Or do we seek knowledge?
And if knowledge what will knowledge accomplish?
Perhaps jumping back in forth will gain us nothing,
Except for the delight of striving.

RECESSES OF THE MIND

In the dark recesses of the mind
Are hidden things both mundane
And of great, albeit unknown, worth

Always there are strange hints
Of something
Or is it nothing?
Always on the edge of consciousness

What is required to bring forth
The profound into the conscious
So that it can be expressed?
And acted upon

FLEETING TIME

Yesterday, today and tomorrow
Time is so ephemeral
What is said now is past
And is part of history

Impossible to hold or feel
For even a second
Yet we remember tomorrow
What we thought today
And speculate about next week

THE HIDDEN PERSONA

Looking into a mirror
We see our selves as others see us
But can they look beyond
The surface persona?

And what is there?
Do we ourselves know
All that lies below?
And in what ways does
The hidden persona express itself?

We go about our daily lives
In a repetitive manner and
Seldom express beyond
The required
How do we - or can we unlock
What ever else is there?
- or do we want to do so?

Is the hidden persona
Ordinary or hateful?
Or is it something that all
Can exalt in and is worth
Bringing forth
But can we do so?

TOWARD OBLIVION

Hurtling toward oblivion
At an ever accelerating pace
We stop at times to think of life past .

I did so first some forty years ago
And marveled then at how quickly
Events had come and gone.

Since then each time I stop and think
Of time past I realize that my life is
Rapidly slipping by uncontrollably
And I wish that I could stop
And savor days and weeks.
Yet to stop now would for me mean oblivion.

So we go on ever nearer to nothingness
And when this time is reached,
I hope it can be said that
I lived a life worth living.

OVER THE HORIZON

In my mind I see beyond the far horizon
As if I possess personal over horizon radar
I see far shores a half world away
I see old friends, past loves, casual acquaintances
Beaches, hills, mountains, forests, deserts

I smell the distant flora, the beginning rain
I see the bustling cities, the quiet towns
Shopping centers, splendid houses,
Also slums, *favelas,* shanty towns
All the world has to offer
I imagine Queen Elizabeth Market
In Melbourne and the short tram ride to it.

It is, thus, that I can see all places
In my past and can imagine how acquaintances
Are now going about their daily lives
And how the waves still pound onto the
South Victoria Coast

DESERTS OF THE MIND

I see a car speeding down a dirt road
Sending clouds of dust rising into the air
Behind the vehicle and then
Slowly falling back to earth
All in a desert of my mind

Distant purple mountains
Give a strange aching and longing
For places and people unknown
In the desert of my imagination

Searching, then, for clues to where I am
And where I am going
I see but the dryness of the desert
And the mystic of the distant mountains
Fog my mind as the car's dusty clouds
Obscure the past

Are there other places in my mind?
Or only the barren deserts devoid
Of meaningful thoughts

Surely there are valleys and plains
Of verdant life and conscious meaning
Not obscured by the desert's daze
Yet deserts of the mind persist
And we are forced
To find our way within them

THE ESSENCE OF ONE'S BEING

The essence of one's being
Follows us throughout our lives
Does it change as we travel
Our life's course?

Or does it remain forever fixed
Following us, but not partaking
Of new encounters and ideas
And ignoring all growth of being

And what is one's essence?
Is it ephemeral?
How can we define it
In terms we can understand?

Yet it is always present
And friends and family
Somehow recognize it
And may talk of our essence.

Is our essence the same as our being?
Is the essence a superficial part of being?
Certainly the essence is what others
Perceive us to be.
But is it our true being?

FROZEN IMAGES

In one's memories frozen images of time, recede,
But reappear as one lays thinking
Of distant joys, sorrows and loves.
Of the walk I took some sixty year's ago
On a sun drenched Sierra day,
Of an injured son more than twenty years ago,
Of a love affair fifty five years ago
Or one five years ago.

I love to think of past accomplishments
And relive them in my mind.
I regret mistakes and lost loves
But endlessly relive them,
And pretend that I made better judgments.

I think often of my father with a wide brim hat
With a kerchief under it,
For the purpose of repelling mosquitoes,
As he sought a trout from some high mountain lake.
I think of him riding a tractor while cultivating land.

I think of the birth of my children
Those many years ago.
I think of them growing up and having children.
I think of an alpine lake in Wyoming, remote,
With flowers lining its shore,
Or of a vista in Australia
Dominated by eucalyptus trees.

Or the Australian tropical rain forest
With such clear rain forest streams

I think of Tasmania and the waterfalls
And the button grass plains
And of the marsupial cats frolicking around the huts
I think of the dry Flinders Ranges
With native cypress pines
And of the myriad of ants and centipedes
On a hot summer day
I think of New England National Park
And the cloud forest with the moaning rock
And of the great waterfalls
Falling off the New England Plateau.

I think of a backpack in the Sierra Nevada
When my son completely out walked me
Through gorgeous mountains and by sky blue lakes.
I remember backpack trips in the Rocky Mountains
In the Bob Marshall,
In the River of No Return Wilderness
In the bald mountains of Central Nevada
Walking along a trickling stream
In the low velt of South Africa
Watching the large animals.
In the Western mountains
Watching the rock pikas busy
Making their hay stacks

I think of the amazing Icelandic landscapes
Of volcanic flows, some still aglow.
I think of the remarkable Tasmanian landscape,

Cradle Mountain and the countless
Lakes of the Central Plateau

I think of *Porto Alegre* and the bustling squares
And flee markets, farmer's market and parks,
Of the elegant shopping centers
With such beautiful women,
And of the nearby mountains with the resort towns
And parks and water falls and *Parana pines*
Of *Itaimbizinho*, the crack in the mountains
With waterfalls falling into it
Of the *Santa Catarina* beaches
And of the great *Cataratas do Igauçu*
So beautiful it can't be described.

I think of Rio and the worship of the physical,
The beaches, the forest, the lagoon, the buildings,
The joggers, the soccer players,
The volley ball games
And, above all, the beautiful women everywhere,
All with the flaunting rich and the terrible *favelas*

I remember *Ouro Prèto* with the coble stone streets
With the many great churches containing
Incredible gold objects and paintings
And the wonderful inhabitants
Of mixed ancestry
And where it is always spring
And a world heritage site.

I contemplate things of 65 years ago
The first trip to upper Bishop Creek

Of the fishing in Lake Sabrina for small trout
Of the long walk with my father over Piute Pass
Of the first look at Humphrey's basin
And Goethe Lake with large golden trout
Swimming in the shallows.
Then later that summer the long backpack
To Buena Vista Crest, Crescent and Johnson Lakes
And of my father catching large trout.
This seems as yesterday, not 65 years ago.

I think of the Western Cape in South Africa
The many runs and walks on Table Mountain
Of the Bushmen paintings in the Cedarberg
And on farms north of the Cedarberg
Near Ceres and elsewhere
And of the farms with citrus, stone fruit,
Roiboss and grapevines supplying small wineries
Of the vineyards with towering peaks nearby
Of the Drakensberg in Natal and bushman paintings

Of the many races and mixtures
Of the beautiful city of Cape Town
The spectacular University of Cape Town
The Finboos and multitude of flowers
Erica and *Protea* species
Extending northward toward Namaqualand
And eastward into the Karoo and the Little Karoo
Green Point, the valleys
And streams of Table Mountain

I think of the arctic and stunning vistas
Of rivers and lakes and artic animals

All adapted to the tundra
And horrendous cold
In the Brooks Range in Northern Alaska
Or in Sammarland in Northern Sweden

The trek and camping in the Brooks Range
Or the comfortable huts along the
Kings Way path in Sweden
Perhaps with a sauna
And always with the friendly Swedes

I see an image of the stone Presidents
In the Black hills of South Dakota
With Horse Thief Lake close by
And further into the Hills
The springs at the head
Of the Roads Fork of Rapid Creek
And the fall color of aspens
Along Spearfish Creek
And of the Homestake mine workings not far away

Misty Moon Lake, shimmering in the sunlight
In the Cloud Peak Wilderness of Wyoming
Further along, Lake Solitude
And Wilderness Canyon
Dominated by the Black Tooth
Elsewhere the Lost Twin Lakes beckon
To the North Highland Park and Hallelujah
Dominating the skyline
Nearby, Lake Geneva and Lake Elsie
All magical and mystical

The Alaska Kenai
Resplendent with glaciers, lakes and rivers
With forests and magnificent coast
Small towns Hope, Seward, Homer
The inlets, the paths of beauty
Abounding and everywhere wildness

The Adelaide Hills covered with Red River Gums
And bush with spines
Or grazing land with eucalypts and grass
Morialta Conservation Park
With seasonal water falls
And Warren Conservation Park
With the water fall on the South Parra
With wallabies, echidnas,
Red bellied black snakes, galahs
Or Cleland National Park
With waterfalls, native bush,
Nature Preserve and Mount Lofty
Further South the Fleureau Peninsula
And Cape Jervis
With Deep Creek Conservation Park
With views to Kangaroo Island
And the Southern Ocean with Dolphins
Playing off shore.

Further North I remember Mount Remarkable,
Mambray Creek, Aligator Gorge
With Melrose at the base
Of the Southern Flinders Ranges
With wallabies, emus and ants beyond count
Native cypress pine, eucalypts and prickly bush

Further North the Central Flinders
And Wilpena Pound surrounded
By jagged peaks and alive with birds
Galahs, King Cockatoos, Green and Red Parrots
Kangaroos and Wallabies abounding
And the Heyson Trail continuing.
All north of agriculture

Wilson's Promontory, the Southernmost
Land in mainland Australia and magnificent
The temperate rainforest with tree ferns
Along numerous streams and the many coves

The Australian Alps with land above tree line
With snow gums at tree line
Rivers and streams everywhere
Heavy winds at times, coarse grass

I remember many weekend walks
Near Melbourne with the Bushwalkers
Or alone near Marysville
Or at Healdsville Sanctuary
With Platypuses, Echidnas, Tasmanian Devils

Many years ago
I back packed with family
In Central Idaho
There were lakes and streams
With multitudinous trout

All was very wonderful
And inspiring
But what I remember most
Is the last day
We planned to camp halfway
To the trail head
But my two youngest children
Kept egging us on
We walked twenty miles
With backpacks
Since it turned out
They were tired of camp meals

The wonder, when I was a
Graduate student in Cambridge
That I was walking where many of the great
New England writers had tread
And of the first colonists at Plymouth Rock
Of the Mayflower
Of the witch hunts in Salem

I think of December 1941
When I was a high school freshman
Four days before my birthday
Pearl Harbor Occurred
I remember students of Japanese Ancestry
In my class
Seeing them waiting with their parents and siblings
To be transported to Concentration Camps

A harsh lesson to be learned about fear
And its consequences

In terrible treatment
Of innocents

A magical trip to Banff National Park
Two weeks in the wilderness
With waterfalls and lakes and hanging glaciers
A climb to near the top of Mount Willingdone
Fords of many rivers and creeks
Then back to civilization
In Banff township

Starting Doctoral studies at Stanford
Moving to married student housing
With my wife and three children
Then my wife also staring her Doctoral studies
My two oldest in first and second grade
My youngest in preschool.
Although tense at times
A happy time with all striving

More travels in the High Sierra
Mineral King to Kings Canyon
The Rae Lakes Loop
Across the Kings-Kern Divide
All swinging in sunlight

I remember my church wedding fifty years ago
With many of my wife's relatives present
And my parents and sister having to
Overcome cancelled trains and flights
Because of storms on the West Coast

More recently I remember my wedding
To my second wife only five years ago
At a Reno wedding chapel with my
Daughter and grand daughter
And Vicki's daughter as witnesses

Both weddings major events in my life.

These and thousands more remembrances
Come rushing back to me,
And the ones sixty five year's ago
Are just as clear as those of last week.
Thus we grow old,
Putting one's memories in order
While thinking of all past events
Yet looking for more adventures
That may appear tomorrow or next year.

END NOTES

[1] The Flathead Alps are a small group of peaks in the Bob Marshall Wilderness, Northern Montana)
[2] The Drakensberg is a rugged mountain range forming the western boundary of Natal-Kwa Zulu with Lesotho. There are great cliffs leading to a plateau at the boundary. Below the topmost cliffs is a contour hiking path running along the base of the cliffs. At one time the area was occupied by native bushmen who painted three tone paintings in many of the area's caves.)